BRUCE GOLDSTONE

100 ways to celebrate 100 days

HENRY HOLT AND COMPANY • NEW YORK

one two three four five six
thirteen fourteen fifteen sixt
twenty twenty-one twenty
twenty-five twenty-six twenty-seven
thirty-one thirty-two thirty-
thirty-six thirty-seven thirty-
forty-two forty-three forty
forty-six forty-seven forty-eight
fifty-one fifty-two fifty-three
fifty-six fifty-seven fifty-eight fifty
sixty-one sixty-two sixty-three
sixty-six sixty-seven sixty-eight sixty
seventy-one seventy-two seventy-
seventy-five seventy-six seventy-seven
eighty eighty-one eighty-
eighty-five eighty-six eighty-seven
ninety-one ninety-two ninety
ninety-six ninety-seven ninety-eight

seven eight nine ten eleven twelve
een seventeen eighteen nineteen
-two twenty-three twenty-four
twenty-eight twenty-nine thirty
three thirty-four thirty-five
eight thirty-nine forty forty-one
-four forty-five
forty-nine fifty
fifty-four fifty-five
-nine sixty
sixty-four sixty-five
-nine seventy
three seventy-four
seventy-nine
seventy-eight
two eighty-three eighty-four
eighty-eight eighty-nine ninety
-three ninety-four ninety-five
ninety-nine one hundred

Ready. . . . Set. . . .
Celebrate!
It isn't just any day—
it's your 100th day of
school. Here are ONE
HUNDRED WAYS you can
celebrate this happy day.

Brush 100.

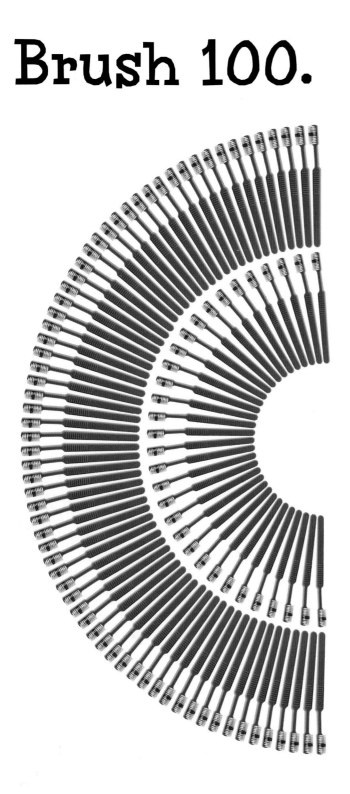

1 Wake up in the morning and brush your teeth with 100 strokes.

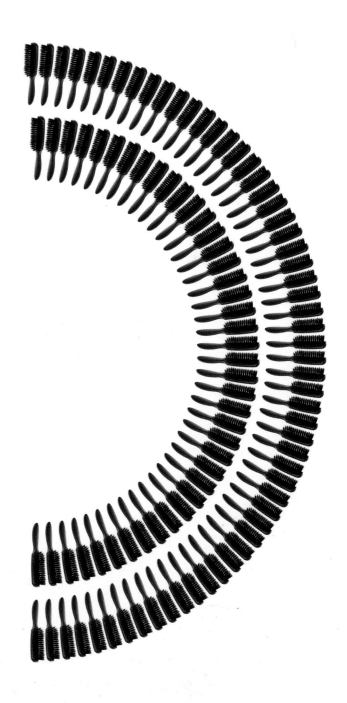

2 Before you go to bed, brush your hair 100 times. (Or maybe you have a patient dog or cat you can brush, or a doll or teddy bear that needs some grooming.)

1 2 3 4 5 10 20 30 40 50

Build 100.

3 Build a shape
with 100 sticks.

4 Build a shape
with 100 blocks.

5 Build a shape
with 100 bricks.

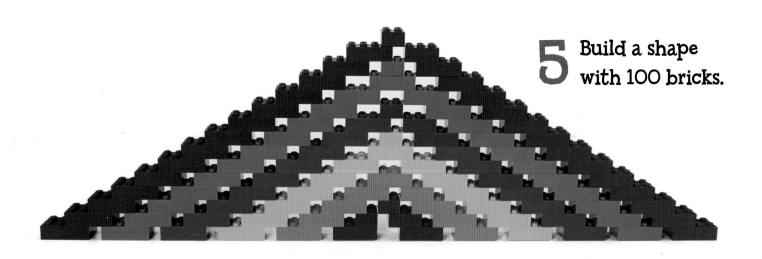

60   70   80   90   100

Link 100.

6 Link 100 paper people.

List 100.

7 Make a list of 100 things. You might list foods, names, animals, or places.

Argentina The North Pole Zanzibar
Machu Picchu Neptune Broadway
Antarctica Los Angeles Mount Rushmore
Trinidad Milwaukee Lake Erie
The Appalachian Trail Seoul
Earth California Finland Portugal
Pago Pago Honolulu Newfoundland Saturn
China Sahara Desert The Nile River
Gulf of Mexico Orange County
Wyoming Atlantic Ocean The Louvre Museum
The Hoover Dam Costa Rica Egypt
Asia Manila Mediterranean Sea
My Backyard Loch Ness The Colosseum
France Greenland
Lake Huron Madagascar Sea of Tranquillity
Mercury Venezuela Central Park
Mount Fuji Alaska Cape Cod

Poland Jupiter Empire State Building
Galapagos Islands Amazon Rain Forest
The Universe The Grand Canyon
The Pyramids of Giza Stonehenge Montreal
Delhi Lake Erie Mars Bunker Hill
Niagara Falls Taj Mahal Walden Pond
Pluto Mississippi River The Rocky Mountains
Lake Superior Thailand The Eiffel Tower
Mount Everest The Equator Pacific Ocean
Venus The Milky Way The Vatican
Detroit Rio de Janeiro Ireland
Florida The Great Barrier Reef Iceland
San Diego Zoo 1600 Pennsylvania Ave. Cape Town
Easter Island Denver New Hampshire
Under My Bed Main Street Mount Vesuvius
Spain The Parthenon Chesapeake Bay
Downtown Lake Victoria Yosemite National Park

Loop 100.

8 Make a chain with 100 paper loops.

Lick 100.

9 Lick a lollipop 100 times. How much will be left?

String 100.

10
String 100 cereal loops to make a tasty necklace.

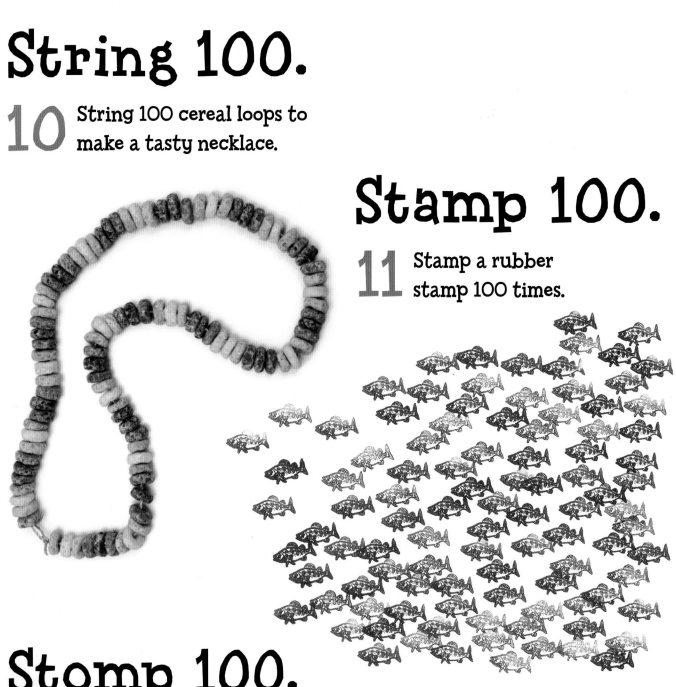

Stamp 100.

11
Stamp a rubber stamp 100 times.

Stomp 100.

12
Stomp a pattern that has 100 beats.

  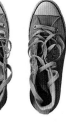   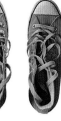  

repeat 10 times

right   left   right   right   right   left   right   left   left   left

10 11 12 13 14 15   20   30   40   50

Stick 100.

13 Stick 100 stickers on a book cover.

Smack 100.

14 Wear lipstick and smack 100 kisses on a poster.

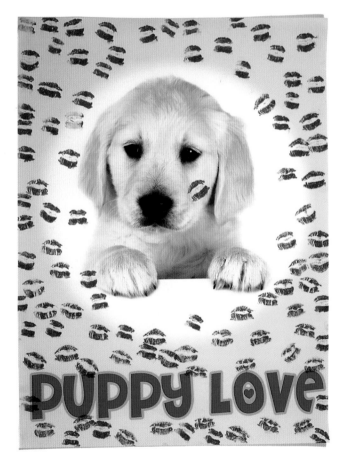

PUPPY LOVE

Stack 100.

15 Stack 100 crackers. Or make a stack of trading cards or CDs.

Count 100.

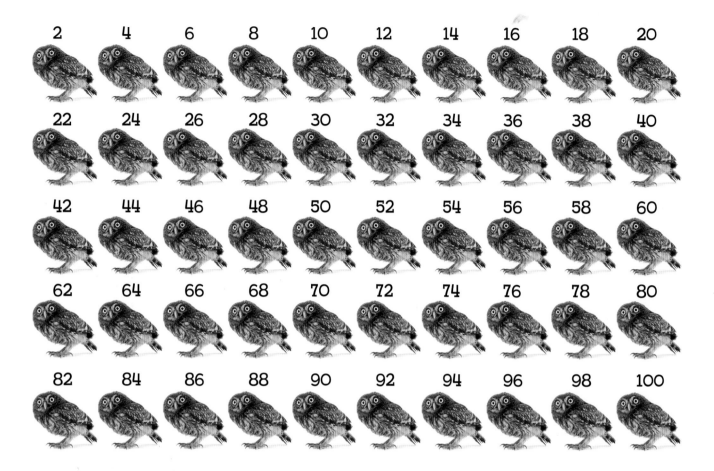

2	4	6	8	10	12	14	16	18	20
22	24	26	28	30	32	34	36	38	40
42	44	46	48	50	52	54	56	58	60
62	64	66	68	70	72	74	76	78	80
82	84	86	88	90	92	94	96	98	100

17 Count to 100 by 4s.
Count legs.

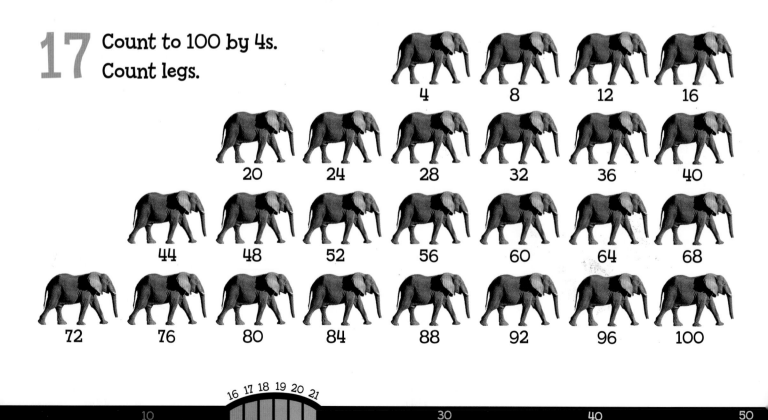

				4	8	12	16
20	24	28	32	36	40
44	48	52	56	60	64	68
72	76	80	84	88	92	96	100

16 17 18 19 20 21

10   30   40   50

Count 100 again.

18 Count to 100 by 5s.
Count fingers.

| 5 | 10 | 15 | 20 | 25 | 30 | 35 |

| 40 | 45 | 50 | 55 | 60 | 65 | 70 |

| 75 | 80 | 85 | 90 | 95 | 100 |

19 Count to 100 by 10s.
Count toes.

| 10 | 20 | 30 | 40 |

| 50 | 60 | 70 | 80 |

| 90 | 100 |

20 Count to 100 by 20s.
Count dollars.

$20 $40 $60 $80 $100

25¢   50¢   75¢   100¢

21 Count to 100 by 25s.
Count cents.

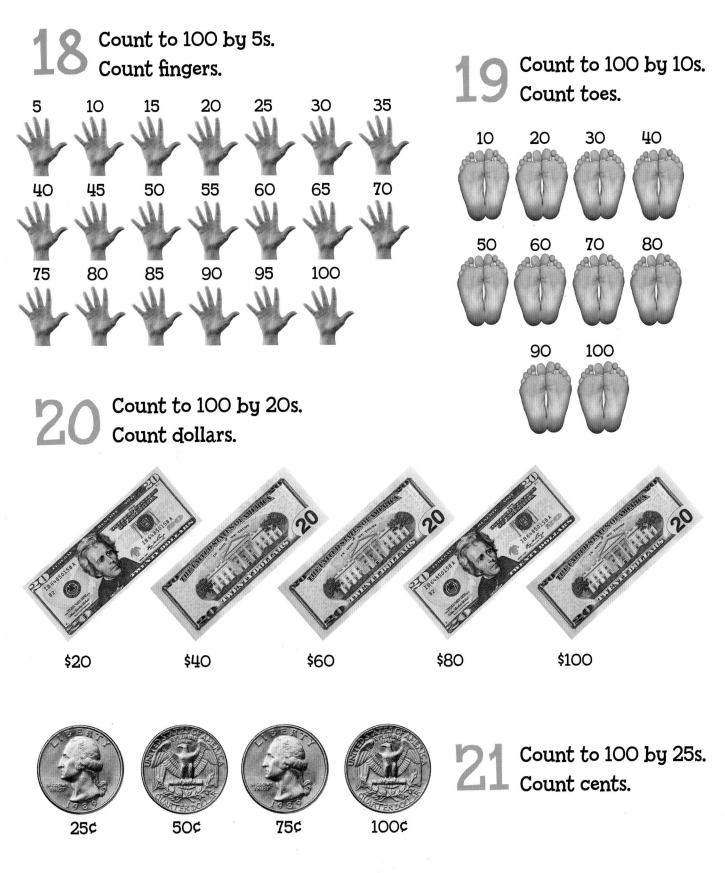

Hop 100.

22 Hop 100 times—on one foot or two feet.

Run 100.

23 Run 100 yards as fast as you can.

START

10   20   30   40

22 23 24 25

10   20   30   40   50

Jump 100.

24 Jump 100 times. You might do 100 jumping jacks. Or jump rope 100 times.

Walk 100.

25 Walk 100 steps in any direction. Guess where you will stop. How close was your guess?

FINISH

50   60   70   80   90   100

60   70   80   90   100

Plant 100.

Plant 100 seeds and wait for them to grow.
Don't forget water and sunlight.

Print 100.

27 Print 100 fingerprints. You can turn them into bugs, birds, and other animals.

Eat 100.

28 Eat 100 pieces of cereal at breakfast.

29 Dine on 100 peas or corn kernels at lunch.

30 Share 100 pieces of pasta at dinner.

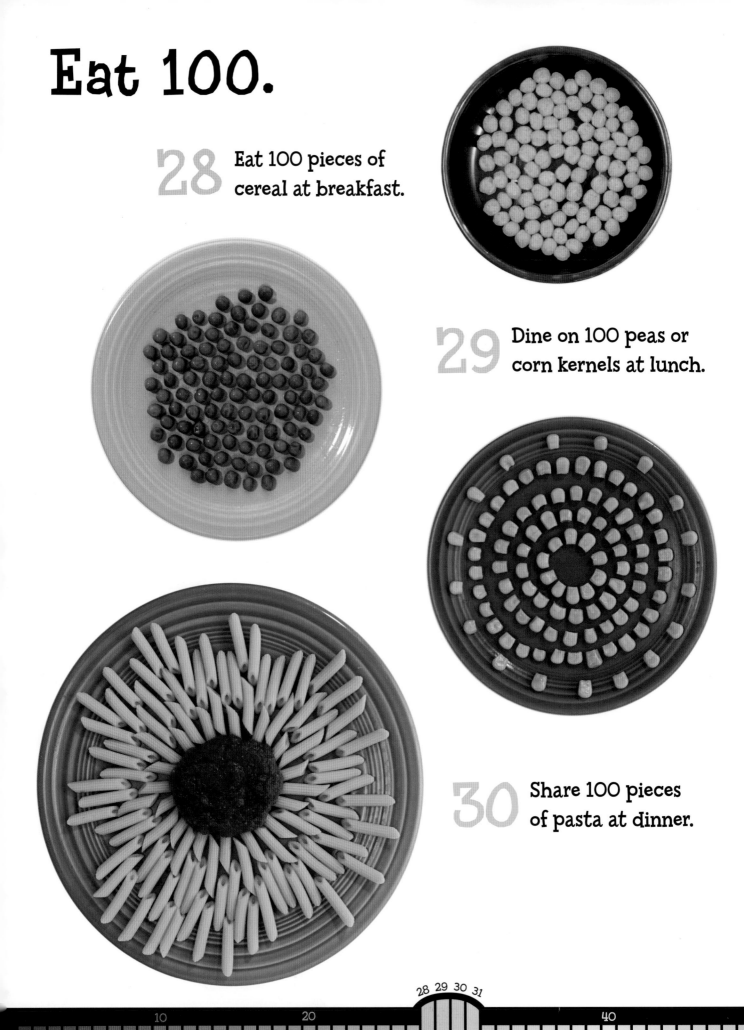

28 29 30 31

10   20   40   50

Eat 100 more.

31 Make a trail mix with 100 bits and pieces. Combine your favorite snacks. Here's one way you can do it. Mix together:

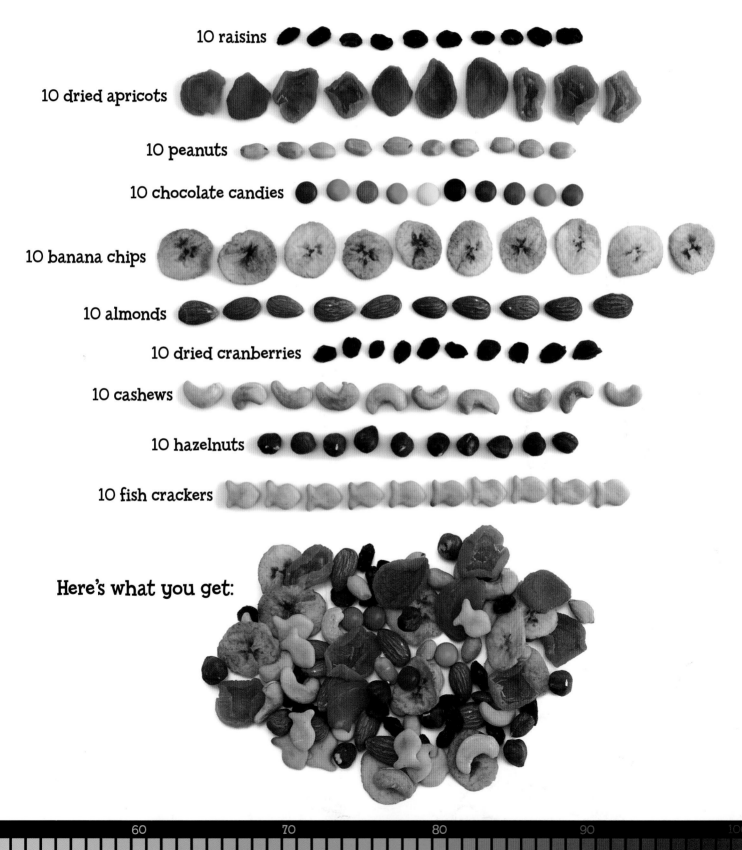

10 raisins

10 dried apricots

10 peanuts

10 chocolate candies

10 banana chips

10 almonds

10 dried cranberries

10 cashews

10 hazelnuts

10 fish crackers

Here's what you get:

Seek 100.

Look for the numbers 1 to 100. Go on a scavenger
hunt. Keep track of the numbers you find.

Snap 100.

33 Find objects that look like the number 100. Snap photos of your best arrangements.

60   70   80   90   100

Draw 100.

34 Draw 100 clouds. **35** Draw 100 birds. **36** Draw 100 waves. **37** Draw 100 people.

34 35 36 37 38 39 40

10   20   30   50

Recycle 100.

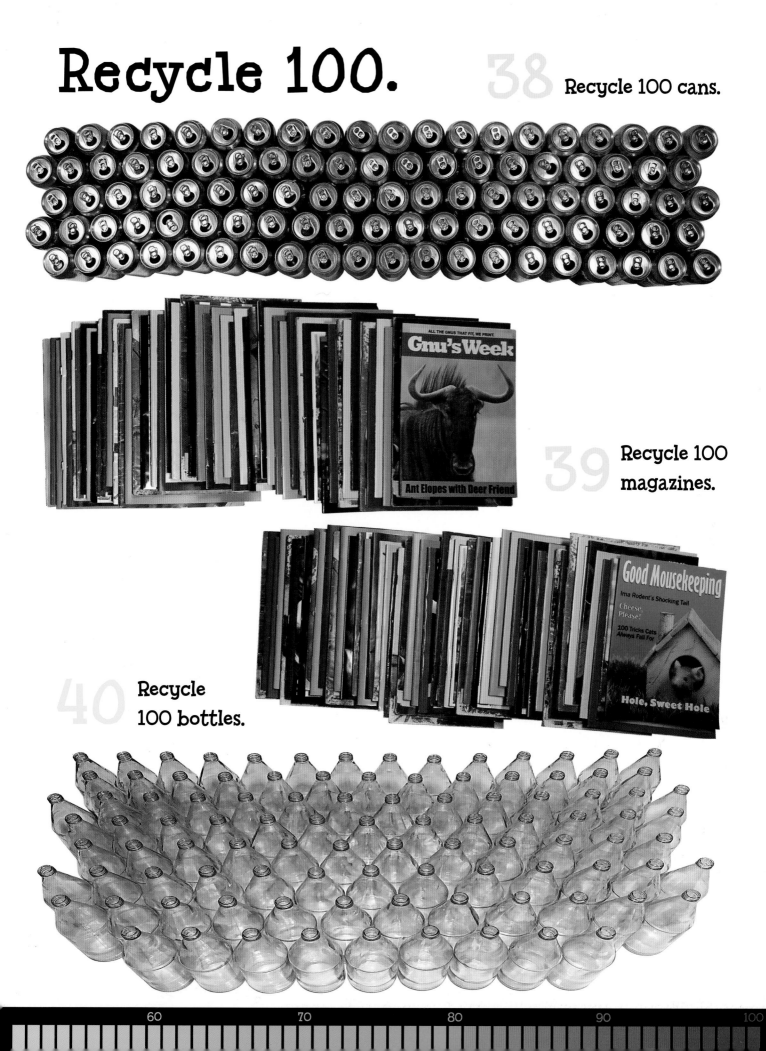

38 Recycle 100 cans.

39 Recycle 100 magazines.

40 Recycle 100 bottles.

Gnu's Week

ALL THE GNUS THAT FIT, WE PRINT.

Ant Elopes with Deer Friend

Good Mousekeeping

Ima Rodent's Shocking Tail

Cheese, Please!

100 Tricks Cats Always Fall For

Hole, Sweet Hole

60   70   80   90   100

Add 100.

Find 100 ways to add
numbers to reach 100.

$1+99=100$ $17+83=100$ $34+66=100$ $51+49=100$ $68+32=100$ $85+15=100$

$2+98=100$ $18+82=100$ $35+65=100$ $52+48=100$ $69+31=100$ $86+14=100$

$3+97=100$ $19+81=100$ $36+64=100$ $53+47=100$ $70+30=100$ $87+13=100$

$4+96=100$ $20+80=100$ $37+63=100$ $54+46=100$ $71+29=100$ $88+12=100$

$21+79=100$ $38+62=100$ $55+45=100$ $72+28=100$ $89+11=100$

$5+95=100$ $22+78=100$ $39+61=100$ $56+44=100$ $73+27=100$ $90+10=100$

$6+94=100$ $23+77=100$ $40+60=100$ $57+43=100$ $74+26=100$ $91+9=100$

$7+93=100$ $24+76=100$ $41+59=100$ $58+42=100$ $75+25=100$ $92+8=100$

$8+92=100$ $25+75=100$ $42+58=100$ $59+41=100$ $76+24=100$ $93+7=100$

$9+91=100$ $26+74=100$ $43+57=100$ $60+40=100$ $77+23=100$ $94+6=100$

$10+90=100$ $27+73=100$ $44+56=100$ $61+39=100$ $78+22=100$ $95+5=100$

$11+89=100$ $28+72=100$ $45+55=100$ $62+38=100$ $79+21=100$ $96+4=100$

$12+88=100$ $29+71=100$ $46+54=100$ $63+37=100$ $80+20=100$ $97+3=100$

$13+87=100$ $30+70=100$ $47+53=100$ $64+36=100$ $81+19=100$ $98+2=100$

$14+86=100$ $31+69=100$ $48+52=100$ $65+35=100$ $82+18=100$ $99+1=100$

$15+85=100$ $32+68=100$ $49+51=100$ $66+34=100$ $83+17=100$ $100+0=100$

$16+84=100$ $33+67=100$ $50+50=100$ $67+33=100$ $84+16=100$

Cut 100.

Cut 100 squares.

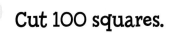
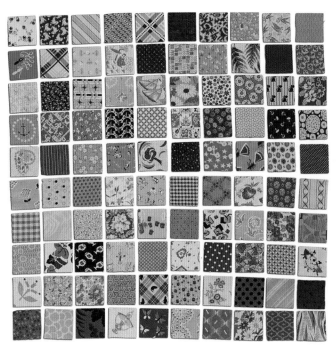

Cut 100 circles.

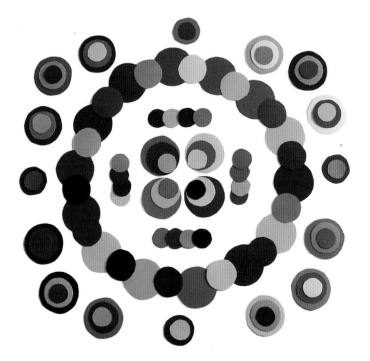

Cut 100 hearts.

Cut 100 triangles.

60   70   80   90   100

Flip 100.

Flip a coin 100 times. How many times will it land heads up?

Clip 100.

47 Clip together 100 paper clips.

Clap 100.

48 Clap 100 times.

Tip 100.

49 Line up 100 dominoes and then tip them over.

Mop 100.

50 Help out at home or school on the 100th day. Mop or sweep a floor in 100 strokes.

Sip 100.

51 Drink a glass of water in exactly 100 sips.

Read 100.

52 Hold a Read-a-Thon with your classmates or friends. How many days will it take you to read 100 books?

Write 100.

53 Write a sentence or a poem that has 100 letters.

If you count very carefully you will surely discover that this sentence contains exactly one hundred colorful letters.

54 Write a poem or story that has 100 words.

Once there was a worm who wanted to be a movie star. Everyone thought that was a really bad idea. The worm did not care. He wiggled all the way to Hollywood.

No one noticed him. It is hard to get attention when you cannot talk. Did the worm give up? Of course not. This is a story about sticking to your dreams, even if you are a worm.

One day, he squirmed his way onto a movie set. Naturally, no one noticed.

When he saw the movie, there he was—next to the actor's foot. He was a star!

Stitch 100.

55 Sew a picture in 100 stitches.

Stretch 100.

56 Touch your toes 100 times.

Plan 100.

57 Plan a zoo for 100 animals.

Pop 100.

58 Pop 100 soap bubbles.

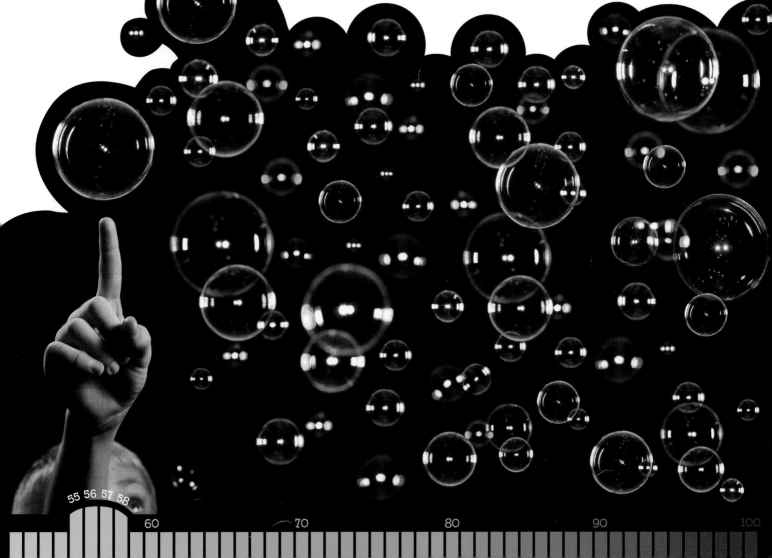

55 56 57 58
60 70 80 90 100

Measure 100.

59 Measure 100 inches. Find something that is 100 inches long.

60 Measure 100 centimeters. Find something that is 100 centimeters long.

61 Measure 100 grams. Use a scale to find things that have a mass of about 100 grams.

62 Measure 100 miles. Use a map to find a place that is 100 miles from your home.

63 Measure 100 seconds. Ask a friend to start timing. Say stop when you think 100 seconds have passed. How close were you?

Melt 100.

64 Melt 100 ice cubes in a large container. Mark a line that shows where you think the water level will be when they're melted.

Collect 100.

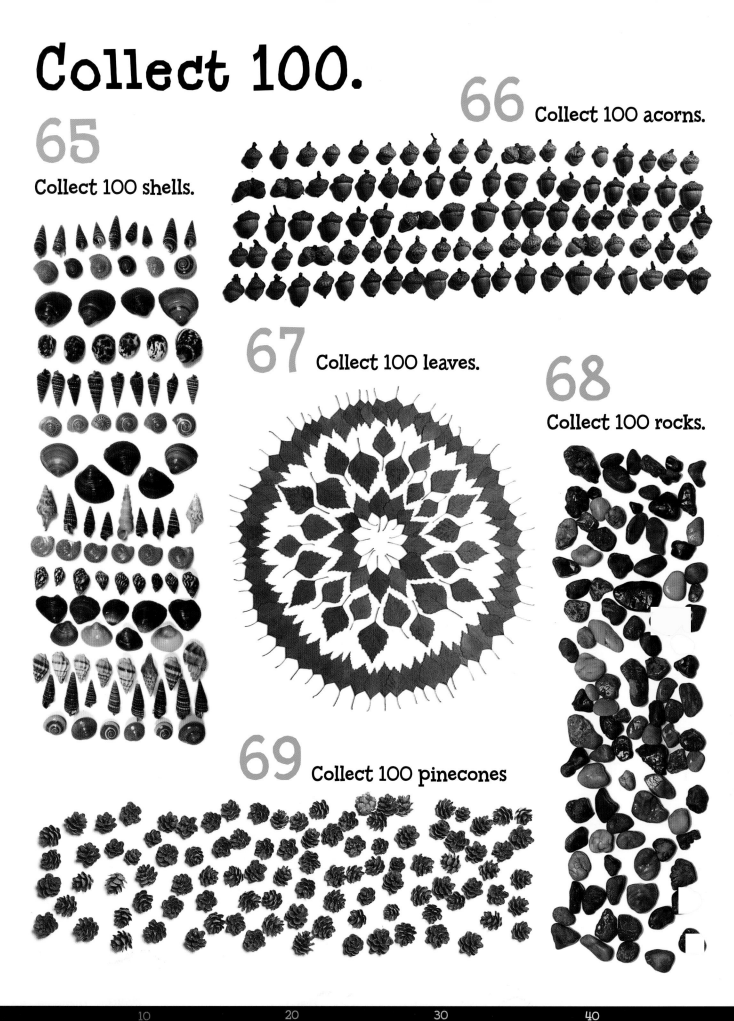

66 Collect 100 acorns.

65 Collect 100 shells.

67 Collect 100 leaves.

68 Collect 100 rocks.

69 Collect 100 pinecones

Collect 100 more.

70
Collect 100 cars.

71
Collect 100 coins.

72
Collect 100 plastic toys.

73
Collect 100 marbles.

74
Collect 100 stamps.

Speak 100.

75 Say **"hello"** in 100 languages.

Albanian **mire dite** (meer DEE-tah)	Amharic **tadias** (TAH-dee-yahs)	Arabic **as salaam-u-'alaykum** (as sa-LAHM-u-alaykum)	Armenian **parev** (pah-REHV)	Basque **kaixo** (kai-SHOW)
Cantonese **wei** (WAY)	Catalan **hola** (OH-la)	Cherokee **o-si-yo** (oh-see-YOH)	Chickasaw **halito** (hah-lee-TOH)	Creole **kushe** (koo-SHEH)
Dzongkha **kuzug zangpo** (koo-ZOOG jahng-POH)	English **hello** (heh-LOH)	Eritrean **selam** (sah-LAH-ahm)	Estonian **tere** (TEH-reh)	Fijian **bula** (MBOO-lah)
Gaelic **dia dhuit** (JEE-ah gwihch)	Georgian **gagimarjos** (GAH-jee-MAR-jos)	German **guten tag** (GOO-tehn tahg)	Greek **geia sou** (YAH soo)	Gujarati **namaste** (nah-MAH-stay)
Igbo **kedu** (KAY-doo)	Indonesian **hallo** (hah-LOH)	Italian **ciao** (CHOW)	Japanese **konnichi wa** (koh-nee-chee wah)	Kannada **namaskara** (nah-mah-SKAH-rah)
Lithuanian **labas** (LAH-bus)	Lokata **tokel niye** (toh-kel NIH-yeh)	Macedonian **zdravo** (ZDRAH-voh)	Malagasy **manao ahoana** (mah-NAH-oh ah-hoh-AH-nah)	Malay **halo** (hah-LOH)
Mandingo **tana mansi** (tah-nah MAHN-see)	Mongol **sainu** (SAH-noo)	Nepali **namaste** (nah-MAH-stay)	Norwegian **hei** (HAY-eh)	Nubi **maskagna** (mahs-kahg-NAH)
Portuguese **ola** (OH-lah)	Punjabi **sat sri akal** (saht SHREE ah-kahl)	Pushtu **eh** (AY)	Quechua **allillanchu** (ah-yee-YAN-choo)	Romanian **buna** (BOO-nah)
Sinhalese **ayuboam** (ah-yoo-BOH-wahm)	Slovak **ahoj** (ah-HOY)	Sosso **inuale** (ih-noo-WAH-lay)	Spanish **hola** (OH-lah)	Swahili **hujambo** (hoo-JAHM-boh)
Tonga **malo e lelei** (mah-LOW EH leh-LAY)	Turkish **merhaba** (MEHR-hah-bah)	Ukranian **vitayu** (vee-TAH-yoo)	Urdu **adab** (ah-DAHB)	Uydur **yakhshimeses** (YAHKH-shee-may-says)

10   20   30   40   50

Bengali **kamon achho** (KAY-mohn AHCH-hoh)	**Bosnian** **zdravo** (ZDRAH-voh)	**Bulgarian** **dobro utro** (DOH-broh OH-troh)	**Cambodian** **jimripsu** (jihm-rihp-SOO-ah)	**Candomble** **sarava** (sah-rah-VAH)
Croatian **bok** (BOHK)	**Czech** **dobry den** (doh-bree DEHN)	**Danish** **hej** (HIGH)	**Dari** **salaam** (sah-LAH-ahm)	**Dutch** **hallo** (HAH-loh)
Filipino **kumusta** (koo-moo-STAH)	**Finnish** **terve** (TEHR-veh)	**Folani** **gam** (YAHM)	**French** **bonjour** (bohn-ZHOOR)	**Fula** **jarama** (JAH-rah-mah)
Hausa **salaam** (sah-LAH-ahm)	**Hawaiian** **aloha** (ah-LOH-hah)	**Hebrew** **shalom** (shah-LOHM)	**Hindi** **namaste** (nah-MAH-stay)	**Hungarian** **szia** (SEE-yah)
Kirundi **amahoro** (ah-mah-HOE-roe)	**Konkami** **marlo** (MAHR-loh)	**Korean** **ahnyung hahsay yo** (AHN-yahng hah-say YOH)	**Laotian** **sabai dee** (sah-BAI dee)	**Latin** **salve** (SAHL-way)
Malayalam **namaska ram** (nah-mah-SKAH rahm)	**Mali** **an sogoma** (ah SOH-goh-mah)	**Malinke** **ini sogoma** (ih-nee soh-GOH-mah)	**Maltese** **merhba** (mehr-hah-BAH)	**Mandarin** **ni hao** (nee HAH-oo)
Nuer **male** (mah-LEH)	**Ojibwa** **aaniin** (ah-NIHN)	**Oromo** **akkam** (a-KAHM)	**Persian** **khoosh amadi** (KHOOSH ah-mah-DEE)	**Polish** **dzien dobrze** (zhehn DOH-breh)
Russian **zdravstvuyte** (ZDRAHST-vooy-tyeh)	**Samoan** **talofa** (tah-LOH-fah)	**Sango** **mbote** (mm-BOH-tay)	**Serbian** **zdravo** (ZDRAH-voh)	**Shona** **kanjani** (ken-john-ee)
Swedish **hej** (HAY)	**Tamil** **wanakum** (wah-nah-KOOM)	**Telegu** **namaskaram** (nah-mah-SKAH-rahm)	**Temne** **topeh** (toh-PEH)	**Tibetan** **tashi delek** (TAH-shee DEH-lehk)
Vietnamese **xin chao** (sihn CHOW)	**Welsh** **hylo** (huh-LOH)	**Xhosa** **sea alafiyah** (say-ah ah-LAH-fee-yah)	**Yoruba** **bawoni** (bah-WOH-nee)	**Zimbabwean** **mkoroi** (m-koh-ROY)

60   70   80   90   100

Guess 100.

76 Start with some rice, beans, nuts, or seeds. Grab a bunch that you think is 100. Then count to see how close you got. Only one group on this page has 100. Which one do you think it is?

(See the last page for the answer.)

Spend 100.

77 Imagine what you would you buy with 100 pennies. (That's $1.)

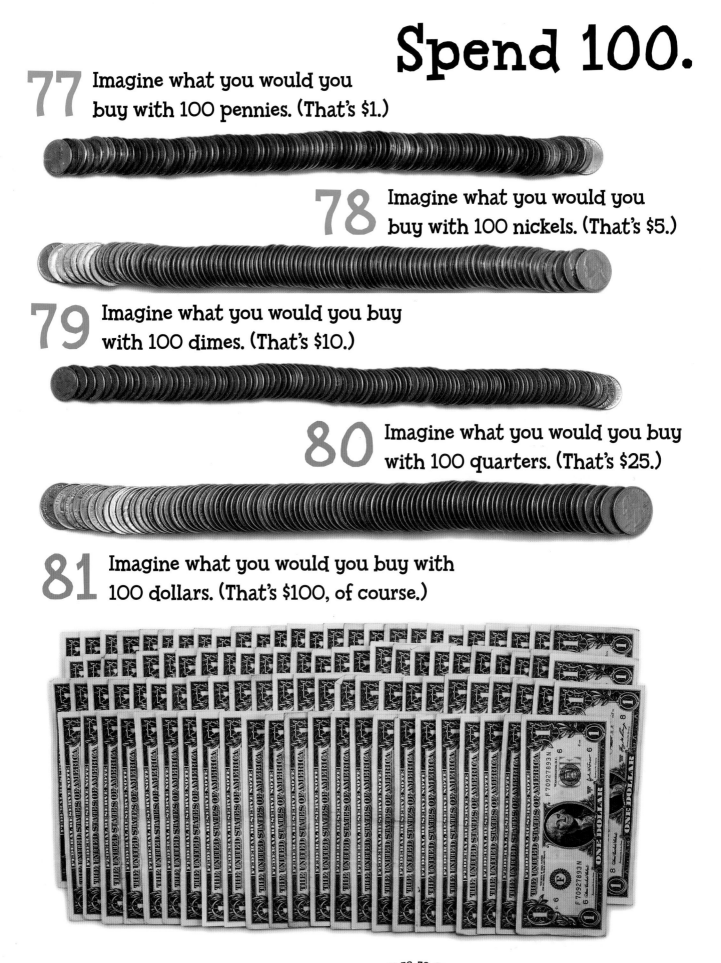

78 Imagine what you would you buy with 100 nickels. (That's $5.)

79 Imagine what you would you buy with 100 dimes. (That's $10.)

80 Imagine what you would you buy with 100 quarters. (That's $25.)

81 Imagine what you would you buy with 100 dollars. (That's $100, of course.)

Make 100.

82 Make 100 legs for a centipede. You can use pipe cleaners.

83 Make a snake with 100 beads.

84 Make 100 quills for a porcupine. You can use toothpicks.

85 Make 100 scales for a fish. You can use buttons.

86 Make a bird with 100 feathers.

Raffle 100.

87 Hold a raffle with 100 tickets. Choose a prize that has something to do with 100.

Jiggle 100.

88 Make a gelatin mold and put 100 berries inside. Or add 100 apple cubes or 100 mini marshmallows.

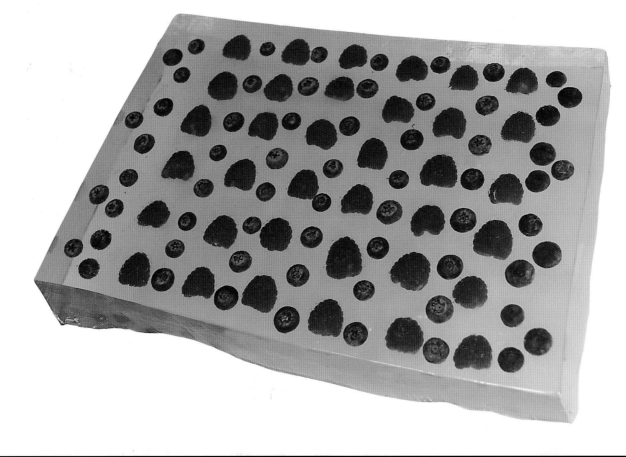

Nibble 100.

89 Pretend you're a bunny and eat a carrot in 100 small bites. Or try a stalk of celery.

Dribble 100.

90 Dribble a basketball 100 times. Or bounce any ball you can find 100 times.

Shake 100.

91 Make a musical shaker. Put 100 beans in an empty can and tape it shut. Shake it as you sing or dance.

Toot 100.

92 Toot a tune with 100 notes. (You can play this verse from "Oh, Susannah" 4 times.)

Oh, Su- san- nah, Oh don't you cry for me, for I come

from Al- a- ba- ma with my ban- jo on my knee.

Bake 100.

93 Make 100 mini cookies.

Predict 100.

FEBRUARY

SUN	MON	TUE	WED	THU	FRI	SAT
	1	2	3	4	5	6
7	8	9	10	11	12	13
14	15	16	17	18	19	20
21	22	23	24	25	26	27
28						

94 Predict what you will be doing 100 days from today. What will the weather be like?

MARCH

SUN	MON	TUE	WED	THU	FRI	SAT
	1	2	3	4	5	6
7	8	9	10	11	12	13
14	15	16	17	18	19	20
21	22	23	24	25	26	27
28	29	30	31			

APRIL

SUN	MON	TUE	WED	THU	FRI	SAT
				1	2	3
4	5	6	7	8	9	10
11	12	13	14	15	16	17
18	19	20	21	22	23	24
25	26	27	28	29	30	

MAY

SUN	MON	TUE	WED	THU	FRI	SAT
						1
2	3	4	5	6	7	8
9	10	11	12	13	14	15
16	17	18	19	20	21	22
23	24	25	26	27	28	29
30	31					

95 Roll a die 100 times. Predict what number you will roll most often. How many times will you roll it?

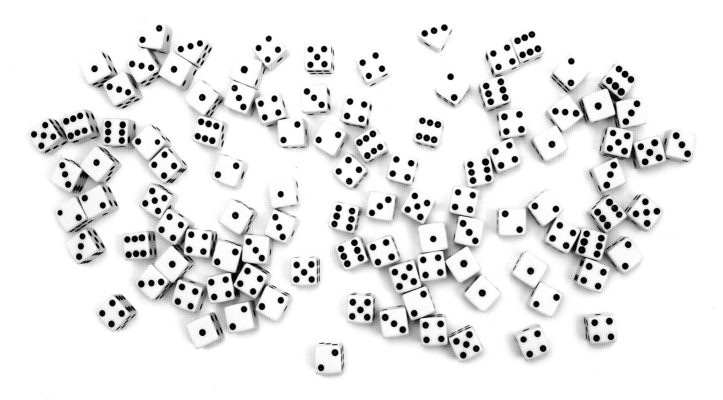

Wear 100.

96 Glue 100 pom-poms on a hat.

97 Pin 100 buttons on a shirt.

Hang up 100.

98 Hang up 100 streamers.

Blow up 100.

99 Blow up 100 balloons.

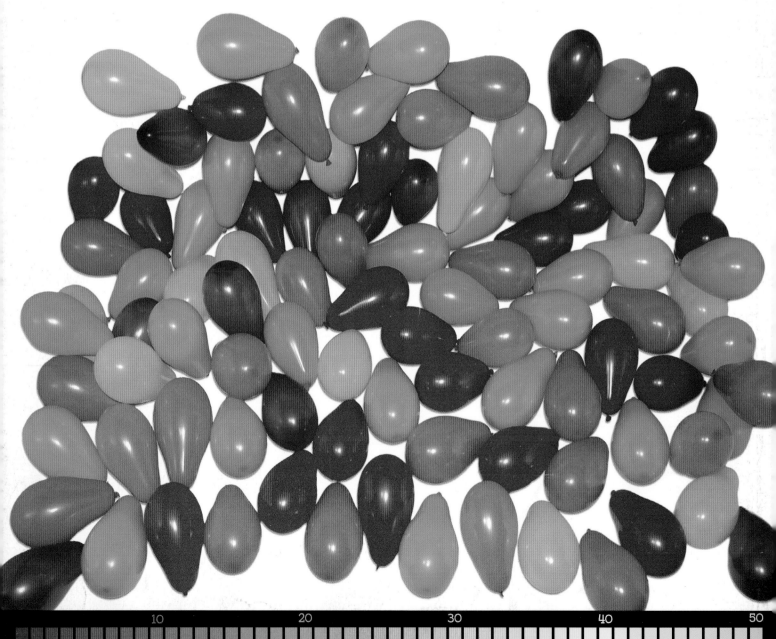

10   20   30   40   50

Blow out 100.

100 Blow out 100 candles.

98 99 1C

60   70   80   90

The 100th day of school can be a fun celebration for the whole family. Some of the ideas in this book require adult supervision. Be careful when lighting candles, using scissors, baking cookies, brushing pets, sewing with a sharp needle, or blowing up a lot of balloons.

Activity Notes

32 You can also make a number collage. Use old magazines and newspapers.

42-45 Cut shapes out of construction paper, foam, fabric, or felt. Or try wrapping paper, magazines and newspapers, or foil.

46 Predict how many times the coin will land on heads. You can also flip 100 coins all at once.

49 Predict how long it will take to set up the dominoes and how long it will take for them to fall down.

75 Not all languages have a word or phrase that translates exactly as "hello." Some of these phrases mean "good morning," "good afternoon," and so on.

76 There are exactly 100 black peppercorns in the lower left circle.

91 Use large beans to create loud shakers. Use rice or lentils for a softer sound.

93 To make 100 mini cookies from a standard recipe, use about 1 teaspoon of dough for each cookie. Reduce cooking time slightly.

95 Make a pictograph or bar graph showing the results of rolling a die 100 times.

For Bobby and his birds (including the one in #86)

All photographs by Bruce Goldstone except the following numbers: 2, 9, 12, 14 (puppy), 16, 17, 18, 19, 20, 21, 22, 26, 46, 50, 51, 53, 56, 58, 59, 60, 61, 63, 89, 90, 94, 98, © shutterstock.com; 48, 89 (bunny), 92, 93 (oven mitt), © istockphoto.com.

Henry Holt and Company, LLC, *Publishers since 1866*
175 Fifth Avenue, New York, New York 10010
www.HenryHoltKids.com

Library of Congress Cataloging-in-Publication Data
Goldstone, Bruce.
100 ways to celebrate 100 days / by Bruce Goldstone. — 1st ed.
p. cm.
ISBN 978-0-8050-8997-4
1. Hundred (The number)—Juvenile literature. I. Title. II. Title:
One hundred ways to celebrate one hundred days.
QA248.G575 2010
513—dc22 2009029320

First Edition—2010 / Designed by April Ward
Printed in April 2010 in China by Macmillan Production (Asia) Ltd.,
Kwun Tong, Kowloon, Hong Kong, on acid-free paper. ∞
Supplier Code: 10

1 3 5 7 9 10 8 6 4 2